PRAISE, APPRECIATION & THANKSGIVING (PAT)

Praise, Appreciation & Thanksgiving (PAT)

Apostle Dr. Victor Adewusi

Apostle Dr. Victor Adewusi Foundation

Contents

Foreword vii
Introduction xi

1. My Major Templates — 1
2. The 3 Powerful J's - Jesus, Jehoshaphat & Joshua — 14
3. Praise, Thanksgiving & Worship Re-Echoed — 20
4. Thanksgiving Days — 32
5. They Also Thanked God — 34
6. More Thanksgiving References — 39
7. The Dangers of Ingratitude — 44
8. Don't Murmur, God Hates it — 50

A Sinner's Prayer 57
About the Author 59

Copyright © 2022 by Aposle Dr. Victor Adewusi

All rights reserved. No part of this book may be used or reproduced by any means, graphics, electronic, or mechanical, including photocopying, recording, taping or by any information storage retrieval system without the author's written permission except in cases of brief quotations embodied in critical articles and reviews.

Scripture quotations marked NLT are taken from the New Living Translation. Copyright © 1996, 2004, 2007 by Tyndale House Foundation. Used by permission of Tyndale House Publishers, Inc., Carol Stream, Illinois 60188. All rights reserved.

Author: Apostle Dr. Victor Adewusi

ISBN: 978-1-989099-19-3 (hardcover)
ISBN: 978-1-989099-18-6 (ebook)

First Printing, 2022

Foreword

Simply put, dad was an amazing man. He taught me how to be a human being first, then a son, a brother, a father and a friend to those in need. Who I am today would not have been possible without his influence in my life. Thus, it is a huge pleasure to write the foreword for one of five books he wrote shortly before being called to glory on August 21, 2021. Without a doubt, dad knew God was calling for him and that his time on earth was winding down. As a result, he began putting his affairs in order. Despite the fact that he was supposed to be on vacation and resting from his hectic ministerial work, he feverishly worked on completing five books within the span of a few months. It is my belief that it was the Holy Spirit that inspired the writing of these books, and dad was merely the willing vessel God used to bring these books to life. This is the only explanation for how he was able to accomplish such an incredible feat in a short amount of time. Therefore, by picking this book up, know that the message and tools contained therein have not been written by a man but rather under the unction of the Holy Spirit. And so, it is my prayer that your life will be forever changed for the better in Jesus' Name.

Praise, Appreciation & Thanksgiving (PAT) is a state of mind that dad embodied. If there is anyone equipped to write on such a topic, it is undoubtedly dad. Ever since I could remember, PAT was a part of our household. Dad taught my siblings and me the value and importance of giving praises, having an appreciative heart and always giving thanks. He also taught us that God cherished these three things, and man valued them as well. Not one to speak empty words, dad lived what he preached. While growing up, I always witnessed dad praising us whenever we did anything positive. This could be as simple as us successfully accomplishing a chore for the first time or as big as making the honour roll in school. Whatever it was, dad never failed to shower praises on those around him. More importantly, he always praised God no matter what the situation was. In good times and not-so-good times, dad never let a day go by where he did not praise God. In fact, the very first prayer dad taught us was the "Lord's Prayer," and the first verse says, "our Father who art in Heaven, hallowed be thy name."

Dad was the one who encouraged me to play the saxophone. When I was starting out and unsure of my skills, dad would encourage and cheer me on. He never made me feel as though I was wasting my time. Perhaps if he hadn't done so, I would have long given up on the saxophone. Dad would shed tears while in worship and whenever he heard me playing the saxophone. To the glory of God, I've been privileged to minister around churches, and I honoured him with a rendition of his favourite songs during his funeral. I believe he was looking down from heaven with a huge smile on his face. His heart was pure, and it was amazing to learn several life skills under his tutelage.

Dad embodied the same attitude towards being appreciative and giving thanks. You could give him a pair of shoes, and he would thank you as though you gave him a brand new Tesla. That's just the calibre of man he was. While growing up, there was a period in our lives when our financial situation was not as it ought to be, yet not once did I hear dad complain, and no one ever knew what we were going through. Instead, he always endeavoured to show appreciation whenever someone did something for him personally or for the church; and he always gave thanks to God. Throughout his life, dad also used his personal financial resources to show his appreciation towards those giving their time in service to God. He always preached to us the importance of showing appreciation and giving thanks. He would always tell us how important it was to give thanks to people whenever they did good deeds for us and to God, regardless of the situation. He always instructed us to thank them again the next time we saw them. Many a time, people have failed to show their appreciation for good deeds done for them and, as a result, making it difficult for people to help them. You see, the art of PAT has the power to unlock blessings, lift one out of depressive thoughts and realign one back to what matters most.

The Bible stressed the importance of being thankful and that God inhabits the praises of his people. We sing a song in my language translated thus as "praises are His food, praises are His food, He doesn't eat vegetables, he doesn't eat any meals, praises are His food." When God healed the ten lepers, only one returned to give thanks. The Bible records that the one that came back was the only one who received full and permanent healing. There are numerous examples of giving thanks in the Bible. It does not have to be a grand gesture, as a simple "thank you" goes a very long way.

Dad embodied PAT to the extent that his very last service in church was one in which he had a special thanksgiving service. During his last Sunday in the church, he danced like he had never danced before. Everyone was amazed and wondered what made him so happy and peaceful. At the end of his dance, he gave the church a heartfelt thanks for loving him, standing by him and cheering him on. This was the last memory most people had of him. Although I was not physically present during his last Sunday in church, the reports I received filled me with joy and awe of God because he left the church with an image of him showing PAT.

I will never forget all the lessons you taught me. May your lovely soul continue to Rest in Peace.

Ebenezer Adeshola Adewusi

Introduction

To God alone be all the glory and adoration for giving me the uncommon grace to write this book.

I grew up to learn, know and develop a conscious habit of showing appreciation for any act of goodness that I received, no matter the quantity, the quantum, the quality or even from whom it came, either young or old; great or small; male or female.

Apart from the moral training I got on expressing appreciation to whoever assists me, coupled with most cultures across the world, the Bible is where I will draw most of my inferences. The Bible is the most comprehensive manual of all ages and delves extensively into thanksgiving, praise, and appreciation, which can be seen from Genesis to Revelation.

In this book, I will attempt to slightly deal with the issue of worship, praises, and appreciation as it concerns our Almighty Father, the only maker of heaven and earth.

Many persons, including God Almighty and Jesus Christ, value the act of people expressing gratitude for any form of favour that they have received from others at any time or place.

A wise saying among a particular Nigerian tribe goes, "Whoever expresses an appreciation for a previous act of goodness will surely receive another act of goodness in the future." This saying is true and extremely apt.

Similarly, if you previously rendered financial help to two people and *only* one constantly expresses gratitude while the other never does, who would you be more inclined to assist if you could only help one? Your guess is as good as mine. That is what appreciation does. It is a powerful depth of gratitude both to God and to most men and women.

It is important to show gratitude even to men because even if they don't express their disdain openly, they would remember it whenever that person comes back to them for any assistance.

Appreciation soothes the nerves, and a heart of gratitude opens future doors of assistance. And this advantage is more available to grateful people than those who don't know how to say "Thank you for the other day."

Praises also encourage God and men to offer a helping hand to you whenever the opportunity to do so presents itself.

In Luke 17:12-19, Jesus demonstrated the concept of gratitude, which I will delve more extensively into this chapter later. In the same manner, God told the king of Judah, King Jehoshaphat, to praise Him when the nation of Israel was under attack by three other nations, Ammon, Moab, and Mount Seir. I will delve more extensively into this chapter later. I will also delve deeper into this scripture later in this book.

During His ministry of three and a half years, Jesus Christ told most of the people who he healed to go and show themselves to the people. And to some, He would instruct them not to tell anybody, just as the Spirit ministered to Him. Asking them to go and show themselves to the people meant that He wanted the whole world to know what God had done for them. This display of their healing was an indirect way of showing appreciation to God.

Our Heavenly Father feeds on thanksgiving, praises, and appreciation. In the book of Revelation, there are angels whose only assignment is to worship God without ceasing from morning till evening. I will equally elaborate extensively on this much later.

Outright criticism kills morale if done in the first instance. Therefore, if someone is given a task and makes a mistake, it is advisable to give that person a token of appreciation before correcting them. This approach affects both genders without any exception.

As long as we are still alive, we ought to give to God in any and every circumstance. We must thank Him for the gift of life; thank Him for providing our clothing, shelter and feeding. Are we capable of protecting ourselves from negative influences, both seen and unseen? Or even the frequent spiritual attacks that He keeps away from us? We only give testimonies to Him because we remember the victories that we had in our dreams when we woke up. What about the numerous attacks that we could not remember after waking up?

Praising, appreciating and thanking God can never be exhaustive, and that is why I decided to write this book. Specifically, so that those who don't know what it means to show gratitude to God will begin to do so from the bottom of their hearts.

Many people have lost golden opportunities to experience instant breakthroughs simply because they did not know or consider the essence of appreciation as a significant nugget of growth, development, advancement and progress. After reading this book, may God open your eyes to see the open doors available to those who know the secret of thanking both God and men.

I strongly urge you to buy a copy of this book for your friends, colleagues or family members who are not conversant with the overarching principle of this book so that their lives can immediately begin to experience a positive turnaround.

We must always learn to count our blessings one by one. Our family is our true everlasting love; our friends are our precious jewels; our health is our wealth, and our existence is a priceless gift! We should be grateful and never forget to realize how blessed we are on a daily basis. God appreciates those who honour Him daily with praises, worship, appreciation, and thanksgiving.

According to Psalm 100:4, we should "enter into His gates with thanksgiving, and into His courts with praise; be thankful unto Him, and bless His Name."

God bless you, and happy reading.

1

My Major Templates

For this book, I have decided to draw reference from the story of the ten lepers in Luke 17:12-19 and one of my most significant experiences while in the banking industry.

Praise, Appreciation & Thanksgiving (PAT). PAT equally means showing appreciation or commending people for any good thing they have done. I will treat the issue of the ten lepers and my experiences in the Banking Industry one after the other.

I came across the story of Jesus healing the ten lepers when I was barely nine years old, and it stuck with me till this very day. In fact, it became the major springboard that taught and encouraged me to be grateful for any act of kindness received from anyone. Over six decades, I have heard various dimensions of teaching on the story, which really interests me.

Whether I am right or wrong, I have been privileged to read the Bible from Genesis to Revelation on many occasions, and I have not come across any other situation where Jesus categorically did what He displayed in that particular story.

Jesus Christ was travelling along the border of Samaria and Galilee when the lepers saw Him. They immediately recognized Him and said, "Jesus, Master, have mercy on us." (Verse 13) They received healing instantly, but only one of them came back to show appreciation, according to verses 15-16, which state, "And one of them, when he saw that he was healed, turned back, and with a loud voice glorified God; and fell down on his face at his feet giving Him thanks, and he was a Samaritan." Jesus Christ of Nazareth was greatly amazed, and Verse 17 said, "Were there not ten cleansed; but where are the nine?"

As I mentioned earlier, that singular act of our Savior remained glued to my heart. It revealed the essence of thanksgiving and why we must always show gratitude to our fellow human beings and principally to God, our Creator.

Jesus told the one cleansed leper that came back to show gratitude, "Rise and go; your faith has made you whole." That was a very powerful and authoritative affirmation of permanent healing! Many Bible Scholars have repeatedly confirmed that the healing of this leper was the most spectacular.

Even though it is the best thing to always do, this story has taught me that expressing gratitude is not always easy for most people. Many of them fail to do so at their own peril, albeit in an ignorant manner. How? It could block future channels of assistance or favour towards them. Thus, gratitude is not earned cheaply; it is very hard for many to do naturally. Gratitude requires not just feeling thankful but acting on it and living it out daily.

The only one that came back to glorify God taught us that glorifying God ought to be done openly without shame, and he did it with a loud voice. Hence, God's mercy should cause us to humble ourselves before Him at all times. The Samaritan taught us that faithfulness is demonstrated in two ways- First, the Samaritan knew that mercy came from Jesus and returning to thank Him was a form of faithfulness to the mercy of God that was made manifest in his life. Secondly, the Samaritan's thankfulness for his physical healing showed evidence of deeper spiritual healing, our true salvation.

I got my second template for this book while I was in the Banking Industry in the early 70s. I've referred to this illustration during most of my sermons on thanksgiving as a Preacher both within and outside my country.

Our Branch Manager was of caucasian origin, and for many years, he was fond of buying snacks for many of us whenever it was lunchtime.

Since I cultivated a lifestyle of expressing and showing appreciation during the days of my youth, I readily adopted a habit of returning to my manager's office the following day or whenever I saw him to thank him.

My love for proper dressing was further enhanced during my time as a banker, as we were told that as the first line of contact, we must always portray the good image of the bank to our customers. On a particular Saturday, we went for a weekend assignment that was usually considered "overtime" in those days. Many of us relied on this system to boost our salaries during those days but had since gone into oblivion because I haven't heard any more of it since the early 90s! Nonetheless, our manager would not usually be around during our weekend assignments but decided to come in on that particular Saturday while we were all on the ground floor. He dragged me into his office and instructed me to sit down, then narrated stories of the Bible and shared some things about his personality. During that interaction, I discovered how passionate he was about why someone MUST be thankful. He even told me point blank that he singled me out of the 65-plus employees within the branch because he admired how I appreciated things and my neat appearance.

Before staff members could be promoted, several criteria were considered. I noticed that within a period of six years, most of the staff members, including myself, would receive promotions year after year, except a particular man from the Northern part of our country, who had most of the qualities yet was always left out when our yearly letters of promotion came from the head office. He was always punctual to the office and was very neat and extremely friendly. In fact, no senior officer or any of our supervisors ever complained about him in any way. Since I was familiar with our manager and knew that he would listen to me, I summoned the courage to meet him one afternoon during our break period to express my observation about this particular man.

He told me to sit down and began by asking me if I was familiar with the story of the ten lepers in the Bible that Jesus healed. I responded in the affirmative and even told him where it could be found in the Bible, which greatly inspired him. He said he would not have given me any explanation concerning the matter if the reason had affected me, and I instantly developed visible goose pimples on my face. He continued explaining that the particular man was an ingrate because he was more or less the ONLY staff member in the branch who never said "thank you" or showed any form of appreciation for the lunch packs he typically bought for us. As an emotional person, warm tears instantly began to roll down my face, and I prostrated in his office for having disclosed the reason to me. I immediately pleaded with him to go and inform the "culprit" who was downstairs, and he consented.

I almost fell while rushing down the staircase to inform him. I pulled him aside in the banking hall and narrated my discussion with the manager. He was shocked and completely dumbfounded! He started crying profusely, and after I succeeded in calming him down, we went to meet the manager, who spoke to him exactly the way he did to me. He even asked him if he was familiar with the story of the ten lepers in the Bible, to which he replied "no" because he was not a Christian.

The manager told me to narrate the story of the ten lepers to my colleague, and the implication then took over from me to offer more illustrations to support the one I provided. The man cried so profusely during the ordeal that the manager questioned why he was in such a pensive mood, but he remained speechless. We were both told to leave his office if he was not ready to speak, and it took him almost 8-10 minutes before he could open his mouth to say anything.

The first thing he said was that he usually saw that most staff members were always thanking the manager for one thing or the other, such as the lunch packs for us, but he never saw any need for such a habit! He further disclosed that even while living with his Uncle (his parents died within a three-year interval), he was familiar with people expressing appreciation, but it meant nothing to him!

The manager retrieved his Bible from his drawer and showed him the story of the ten lepers. He was able to convince him that showing appreciation is very essential and that we should make it a culture. Shortly after, he brought out two seized letters of promotion from his drawer and gave him the older one, with the change in his salary and allowance taking effect from that day. As he began to cultivate a habit of thanks and appreciation, he received the latest letter of promotion within four months. He maintained this habit, and by December of that same year, he was promoted again. Since then, all the employees began to call him "Mr 3 in 1"!

He was eventually transferred to another branch but would always purchase my lunch and other occasional gifts during his last five months.

After explaining the incident to his Uncle, he too began buying gifts for me during Easter and Christmas seasons until we lost contact once I left the banking industry. What a lesson!

These two instances became regular reference points for me and reminders that it is essential to cultivate the habit of showing gratitude and appreciation whenever a favour is done for us.

Imagine what the man missed just because of lunch snacks. What would have happened to his promotion if God had not used me to redeem his well-deserved benefits? And he definitely deserved them because he was always topnotch among the criteria for promotion, which were writeable in black and white. But imagine how the branch manager was using his lack of appreciation against him without him being aware.

That brings me to the fore; our Lord Jesus Christ of Nazareth urges us to watch and pray constantly. Thus, on most occasions, our progress in life might not be stalled by negative forces or outside influences but by our own doing.

Many people usually allude to their lack of progress only to misfortune or a satanic attack. The man was praying very well and was used to fasting constantly. He also gave freely and was extremely amiable and loved by almost everybody in the branch. His deficiency, which he never knew, was how to show appreciation. An incident such as this might have impeded many other people's progress, joy, or achievement in other places, but nobody cared to take note of it the way I did.

Thus, showing gratitude goes a long way in our lives, and I want you, my readers, to learn from it. Most people may not go to the extent to which our branch manager went, while others may go even further. What if the branch manager decided to ignore my questions? What if he refused to listen to me? What if he turned me away? I would have simply kept quiet. I want us to keep these two templates at the back of our minds- showing gratitude is essential and opens more doors of favour in the future.

Thanksgiving and gratitude are significant themes throughout the Bible, from the Old Testament straight through to the Book of Revelation.

We praise God to compliment Him and admire Him for all His virtues and who He is. Thanksgiving is usually done to express thanks and gratitude to God for what He has done and provided for us.

People worldwide engage in diverse ways of worshiping and praising their religious leaders. As an extension to worship and prayer, people who believe in God praise Him and give thanks to Him constantly for everything He has done for mankind.

Praising and giving thanks to God may seem similar, yet there is a considerable difference between them. The difference between praise and thanksgiving lies in what we thank or praise Him for, although they both require faith.

Praise is the conscious act of complimenting God for what He truly is and for all His virtues, without any exception. We acknowledge His perfections, works, benefits, and overall excellence when we praise Him. We don't praise Him because of what He will do for us but for who He is. Singing songs, reciting hymns, and praying are ways of praising God. One of my favourite Psalms is Psalm 103:1-5,

> *"Bless the Lord, O my soul;*
> *And all that is within me, bless His holy name!*
> *Bless the Lord, O my soul,*
> *And forget not all His benefits:*
> *Who forgives all your iniquities,*
> *Who heals all your diseases,*
> *Who redeems your life from destruction,*
> *Who crowns you with lovingkindness and tender mercies,*

Who satisfies your mouth with good things,
So that your youth is renewed like the eagle's."

It is a Psalm that I love so much, and from the wordings, one could easily confirm that it aptly captures the essence of thanking Him. Undoubtedly, learning to praise God activates the fullness He has for us.

Thanksgiving is different from praise. Thanksgiving simply means giving thanks to God, not for what He is, but for what He has done for us. We thank Him for the specific gifts and the blessings He has bestowed upon us throughout our life. We could thank God for providing us with good food, a nice home, a wonderful family, and sound health. We can also thank Him for giving us a good job, protection from known and unseen dangers and even for knowing Him as our Lord and personal Savior. The gratitude that comes from our innermost hearts is the core of our thanksgiving.

Praise is more than words. It could be done in the form of singing which is the most popular way of praising God, or by beautiful hymns. However, thanksgiving is merely done by words to show gratitude. It is rooted in the gratitude one has for God, for the things He has been given by God, while praises come from the insight of who God really is rather than gratitude. Though thanksgiving and praises could be distinctly different, they are closely connected because whosoever is praising God is also thanking Him.

In my introduction, I mentioned that I would briefly touch on the meaning of "worship" as far as God is concerned.

The difference between praise and worship may be quite puzzling to some people because they are thought to be used interchangeably. However, people don't realize that there is a significant difference between them. Where praise can be quite distant in nature, worship, on the other hand, is more intimate. Praise means showing your warm approval or admiration of someone, a human being, an animal, or even a deity.

As believers, the heart of a man doesn't need to be near to God for praise to happen. It mostly involves the epithets of the Lord; and involves either giving or receiving something, unlike worship. Any part of nature can praise the Lord, while the Lord does not have any relationship with them. It can also be seen or heard because whoever is praising God cannot be unassuming, and therefore, one can easily determine whether a person is praising or not. On the other hand, man's heart must be near to God whenever worship occurs. Thus, worship brings man closer to God than praise.

Worship is the expression or feeling of reverence and adoration for a deity and brings us closer to the deity more than praise does. In worship, the mind becomes one with the existence of God. Jesus Christ told His disciples that rocks would cry out to worship Him if they would not praise Him. This is so because rocks do not have a relationship with the Almighty. As we worship, our proximity to God is improved and becomes closer. God develops a special kind of relationship with those who worship him with all of their heart and attention. Worship involves both receiving from and giving to God, while praise only involves giving to God.

Worship can be done quietly and is not always seen by the observer. The worshipper alone is conscious of the innate experience. This is an essential difference between praise and worship. Sometimes, however, worship can be visible to the observer, but it does not get as visible as praise.

Finally, praise means showing warm approval or admiration of someone or something. In contrast, worship implies the expression of reverence and adoration for a deity/God. The person who worships God is unassuming, while the one who praises Him is assuming.

Appreciation is whatever we do in recognition and enjoyment of the good qualities of someone or something. It is a complete understanding of a situation or an increase in the monetary value of a particular currency over another currency. It also means gratitude.

We praise God to express acceptance of something that God is permitting to happen. Thus, praising God for difficult situations such as sickness or diseases means that we accept its happening as part of God's plan to reveal His perfect love for us. Remember that we cannot really praise God without being thankful for what we are praising Him for. And we cannot be thankful unless we believe that an Omnipotent, loving and caring father is working for our good. Therefore, praising Him involves both gratitude and joy that God keeps His word to work through everything, provided we love Him (Romans 8:28).

It is, therefore, very profitable to be joyful and keep praying to Him through any situation. And regardless of what happens, we must be thankful to Him, *"for this is God's will for those who belong to Christ Jesus"* (I Thessalonians 5:6-18). Whenever we are going through any circumstance, we should turn it into praise instead of allowing it to weigh us down. Doing so will ultimately weaken and shame the devil and our perpetrators. It is better to always turn dejection to dancing and praise, to strengthen our faith in Christ. Some people may consider that approach to be a stupid one, but as a believer, it is the best option to explore at all times.

Once we understand and apply the technique of praising in place of sorrow, all stumbling blocks in our lives can easily turn in our favour. God is the King of all the earth according to Psalm 47:7, *"Sing praises in a skillful psalm and with understanding."* We are not supposed to push our understanding out of the way or grit our teeth and say, "It does not make sense to me, but I will praise the Lord if that is the only way I can get out of this mess." No. That is not praise but rather a manipulation. We are expected to praise God with our understanding, not despite it.

We must appreciate that our understanding gets us into trouble whenever we attempt to figure out why and how God brings certain circumstances into our lives. We can never understand how and why God does some things, but He wants us to accept with our understanding that He does it. And this is the basis of our praise because God loves us and wants us to sincerely understand that He loves us and that He has a plan for us; Jeremiah 29:11 says, *"For I know the thoughts that I think toward you, says the Lord, thoughts of peace and not of evil, to give you a future and a hope."*

Praising God is not a magic formula for success. It is a way of life that is solidly backed up in God's Word. We praise Him not for the expected results but for the situation just as it is. And as long as we praise God with an eye secretly looking for the desired results, we are only kidding ourselves; and can be certain that nothing will happen to change us or our current situation. Praise is based on accepting the present as part of God's love and perfect will for us. Therefore, praise is not based on what we think or hope will happen in the future. This is an absolute law and clearly observable in the practice of praise. We praise God not for what we expect will happen in or around us, but we praise Him for who He is and where and how we are at the moment.

Let me emphasize that we must not list our heart's desires and then delight ourselves in the Lord in order to get them. We are first to be delighted, and once we have experienced delightment with Him, we will discover that everything else becomes secondary.

God does have a perfect plan for our lives. Despite what we are passing through, we must learn to turn it faithfully to praise. When we do, a solution of unimaginable weight would suddenly surface. We may look at the circumstances surrounding us and think we have been standing still forever in one painful spot. The more we pray and cry for God to help us, the more the circumstances seem to be piling up. The turning point cannot come until we begin to praise Him for our situation instead of crying for Him to take it all.

Instead of asking God to take our challenges away from today, I suggest that we begin to pray thus, "God, I thank you that my life is just as it is. Every situation has been your gift to bring me to the place where I am right now. You would not have permitted any of these things to happen if you had not known that it was best for me. God, I know that you love me. I mean it, God, I know you do love me." Once we cultivate the habit of doing this sincerely, begin to accept our present situation with thanksgiving and remember the contents of I Samuel 16:7, *"Man looks at the face, but God sees our hearts,"* our turning point in life will suddenly surface. Why? God has a perfect plan for our lives, but He cannot move us to the next step until we have joyfully accepted our present situations as part of that plan. What happens next belongs to God, not us.

As they say, "a changed attitude causes changed circumstances." It is simple psychology. When you stop complaining and begin to smile, you feel different; others then start to treat you differently, and your whole life can undergo a dramatic change for the better. Also, there is some logic in the phrase, "smile, and the world will smile with you; cry, and you will cry alone." But praising God is something more than a change in our own attitude. Many of us use the popular phrases "Praise the Lord" or "Thank God" so glibly that we tend to lose sight of their real meaning. There is power in our words of praise to God and in our attitude of thankfulness. But God is Omnipotent and retains absolute control, so we must constantly beat that fact in mind. At times, it is quite easy to fall into the trap of thinking that we have the power to manipulate or change a situation simply by reciting a particular form of prayer.

Whenever we sincerely accept and thank Jesus for a situation, believing that He has allowed it to happen, a supernatural and divine force is released into that situation that causes change beyond our understanding as an unfolding of natural events. Any form of sincere prayer opens the door for God's power to move into our lives, but the prayer of praise releases more of God's power than any form of petition. The Bible is replete with examples that show this fact repeatedly; Psalm 22:3 says, *"But thou art holy O thou that inhabits the praises of Israel."* No wonder God's power and presence are nearer whenever we praise Him. He actually dwells, inhabits and resides in our praises.

2

The 3 Powerful J's - Jesus, Jehoshaphat & Joshua

There are many instances in the Bible where the power of praise was employed by many vessels of God to bring about unexpected miracles. I am, however, greatly inspired to discuss some very potent and remarkable ones so that they can continue to resonate in our lives and hearts for a long time. They include the Ministry of Jesus, the battle fought by King Jehoshaphat of Judah, and Prophet Joshua, the Son of Nun! I will take them one after the other.

1. **Jesus:** If we looked at the prayers of Jesus when he faced difficulties, we would see that He spent more time thanking His Father than He did shouting out in distress to Him.

There was a time, as recorded in Mark 6:41-43 when more than 500 people had followed Him to listen to Him preach. After preaching, Jesus knew that they were hungry, and He did not want them to go back home with empty stomachs, yet the only food available was the one surrendered by one little boy's lunch of five loaves of bread and two fish. He did not ask God to perform any extraordinary miracle while blessing the little boy's lunch. He simply looked up to heaven, and while praising God, He gave thanks, broke the loaves, kept on giving them to the disciples to distribute amongst the people, and did likewise to the two fishes! They were all fully fed satisfactorily. Without counting the women and children among the 5000 that were fully fed, twelve baskets full of broken bread and fish were left over.

Similarly, when Jesus was confronted with the death of His friend Lazarus, He again prayed a simple prayer of thanksgiving. Although He was told that Lazarus' body was already decomposing since he had been dead for four days, Jesus lifted His eyes to God and said, *"Father, thank you for hearing Me,"* according to John 11:41. He then commanded Lazarus to come out of the grave. The man who had been dead for four days walked out! When He got to the grave, He told them to roll away the stone.

The Bible says that Jesus came into this world to make it possible for us to praise God. Even Isaiah the Prophet foretold of His coming and said that he would come to preach the Gospel of good tidings (Isaiah 6:1-3). Once we believe in Him and remember to constantly praise Him in all circumstances, we can easily do everything He did throughout His ministerial assignment that spanned 3 1/2 years. He even assured us that we could do even more, according to John 14:12-13.

2. **(King) Jehoshaphat:** According to 2 Chronicles 20, Jehoshaphat, the King of Judah, woke up one day and suddenly discovered that the powerful armies of three nations (Moab, Ammon, and Mount Seir) had surrounded his little Kingdom. Considering the strength of his army and the size of the tiny country of Judah, Jehoshaphat knew that he would never have the might to confront those that besieged his Nation and overcome them.

A vital step in praising God is to shift our view from the threatening or difficult circumstance and look to God instead. But Jehoshaphat did not just close his eyes to the threat against his Kingdom or pretend that the enemies were not there. He took careful stock of the situation, recognized his helplessness and turned to God for ultimate help. Hence, we are not to be blind to the real threat of the devil in our lives. Seeing threats for what they are giving us greater cause to praise and thank God for working in them with perfect control and authority. It is essential for us not to be preoccupied with the appearance of evil within our midst.

Since God had seen the heart of Jehoshaphat was unwavering and solely dependent on Him, He told him not to be afraid or dismayed because the battle was not his own (2 Chronicles 20:15). God, therefore, assured Jehoshaphat that he would not fight the battle but that he should stand still and see the deliverance of the Lord (2 Chronicles 20:17). We should constantly remember these 2 Bible portions as they apply to the battle that confronted Jehoshaphat on that day. And because his faith was fixed on God, he was given the "way of escape." After consulting with the people, he appointed those who would sing (choristers) unto the Lord and praise Him in their holy garments, saying, *"Give thanks to the Lord, for His mercy and loving kindness endure forever."* (2 Chronicles 20:3). As they began to sing, the Lord set ambushments against the armies that had come against Judah. They were defeated (2 Chronicles 20:22-23). That was the power of praise!

3. **Joshua:** As we segway into the third J under this chapter, we are told of a wonderful and unforgettable story in the Book of Joshua, Chapter 6.

The City of Jericho was a fortified stronghold, and the children of Israel wanted to take the city after they had been wandering in the wilderness for over 40 years. They had no weapons of warfare, and because Joshua was a firm believer, he took the matter to God. He was then instructed to lead the Israelites on a march around the city once for six days and seven times on the seventh day while blowing their trumpets of victory. In the eyes of the uninformed, it would have looked rather absurd, but it was not foolishness in the sight of God. I am sure those watching them must have said in their spirits, "The Israelites are wasting their time." But what happened on the seventh time the trumpet was blown according to God's directive? The great walls of the fortified city crumbled completely!

Three principal factors were unavoidably constant based on the accounts of the 3 Js above: praise, faith and trust in God. Thus, under any situation and irrespective of what we are going through, we must always commit the issue to God's unfailing hands. Let us have faith in Him unfailingly, believing that He is extremely capable of seeing us through any seemingly difficult situation. Additionally, we must constantly praise Him from the bottom of our hearts, knowing that nothing happens without His knowledge. He knew how we got into every situation, and He alone knows how we can get out of it. Come to think of it, have we ever seen a situation where being dejected or downcast solved it? Instead of easing the matter, it would worsen it and could even negatively affect a person's health. Joshua led the children of Israel to magnificently enter the City of Jericho with the Ark of Covenant because they were not terrified but renewed their faith and trust in God.

The will of God in Jesus Christ is for us to be thanking and praising Him constantly according to Psalm 100:4, *"Enter unto His gates with thanksgiving and unto His courts with praise: Be thankful to Him and bless His Name."* Therefore, once we cease to praise God regularly and be thankful to Him, we are out of His will. Apart from being out of the will of God, whoever refuses to thank, appreciate and worship God sincerely is ultimately trying to be out of His grace also. We cannot enjoy God's grace without being thankful, nor can we separate thankfulness from the grace of God.

The apostle Paul equally has various references concerning consistent thanksgiving, from man to God, but I will only cite four of them as shown below. I encourage you, my reader, to emulate his admonitions. I wish to prepare your hearts that in the four instances quoted below, thanking and appreciating our Creator is not an option, advice or suggestion, but rather a command.

1. **I Thessalonians 5:16-18** says, *"Rejoice always; pray without ceasing. In everything give thanks for this is the Will of God in Christ Jesus for you"*.
2. Paul's second command is in **Ephesians 5:18,** *"And do not be drunk with wine in which is dissipation, but be filled with the Holy Spirit."*
3. Paul again gave us another great command in **Colossians 3:15-17**, which goes thus, *"And let the peace of God rule in your hearts to which also you were called in one body and be thankful. Let the Word of Christ dwell in you richly in all wisdom, teaching and admonishing one another in psalms and hymns and spiritual songs, singing with grace in your hearts to the Lord. And whatever you do in word or deed, do all in the Name of the Lord Jesus, giving thanks to God the Father through Him."*
4. **Philippians 4:6** says, *"Be anxious for nothing but in everything by prayer and supplication with thanksgiving, let your requests be made known to God."*

Therefore, in everything we set out to do or accomplish, our apostle encourages us to always do it with thanksgiving in our hearts and in the name of Jesus Christ. Also, as long as we are full of the Holy Spirit, we would be convinced that it is proper always to give thanks to God.

Thus, no matter how we feel or whatever we are passing through in our lives, let us constantly bear it in mind that these three facts are paramount:

1. **God is always good.**
2. **His mercy is from everlasting to everlasting.**
3. **His truth endures through all generations.**

We must, therefore, never concentrate on our feelings or situations except on the unchanging aspects of God's nature and His dealings with us.

Since there are always two sides to a coin, it is therefore very appropriate to briefly look at the opposite aspect and effect of thanksgiving. The Bible calls it "murmuring," which can also be explained as "complaining"! Thus if we are not praising, thanking or worshiping God, it means we are murmuring, and He absolutely hates those who murmur. The Israelites were guilty of this after they were delivered out of Egypt, according to Numbers 21. When they began to murmur against God, He responded by sending fiery serpents among them, and they began to die. Apostle Paul advised us never to be unthankful, as shown in I Corinthians 10:7-10, which says, *"And do not become idolators as were some of them. As it is written, The people sat down to eat and drink and rose up to play. Nor let us commit sexual immorality as some of them did and in one day, twenty-three thousand fell; nor let us tempt Christ, as some of them also tempted, and were destroyed by serpents; nor complain, as some of them also complained, and were destroyed by the 'destroyer."*

3

Praise, Thanksgiving & Worship Re-Echoed

We can approach and relate with God through any of the above, as they relate to a different aspect of God's character:

1. **Through thanksgiving, we acknowledge God's goodness.**
2. **Through praise, we acknowledge God's goodness.**
3. **Through worship, we acknowledge holiness. Worship is the highest activity of the human spirit.**

We cannot enjoy God's grace without being thankful, nor can we separate thankfulness from the grace of God. Thus, whenever we are unthankful, we are surely out of the grace of God. Many of us are in the habit of only thanking God whenever He does something for us, which is wrong. We also grumble when things do not go the way we expect them to go. This comes so easily to some people that we often do not realize what we are doing and tend to forget that this is the exact opposite of thanksgiving. The attitude of praise releases the power of God into our lives and the attitude of murmuring and complaining blocks that power. Resentment, fear, grumbling and complaining cause delays in unfolding God's plan for us. He has a perfect time and plans for us, and we must constantly realize that His own timing does not always coincide with our own expectations; which is a major reason why many people do not usually see why they should praise or thank God regardless of the situations they are passing through. We must always bear in mind that "The joy of the Lord is our strength," according to Prophet Nehemiah 8:10.

It is very instructive to mention that while we praise and thank God for what He has done for us or thank Him with faith in advance of what we believe He will do for us, we worship Him because of who He is. When we thank, praise and appreciate God, He can be on His Throne acknowledging our exhortations. However, whenever we wholeheartedly worship Him, He will automatically leave His exalted Throne and come down to literally join us wherever He is being worshiped.

I wish to shed more light on what happens whenever we sincerely worship God:

1. We see more clearly because His presence becomes more palpable and mysteriously real. Whenever silence is found or seen in our worship, we sense and easily apprehend the mystery of incarnation. It automatically grabs us, and the desire to have more of His presence is felt inside our spirits. The things of this world really do dim in the light of His glory and grace.
2. God automatically invites us to take a step closer to Him, resulting in smoother communication and interaction. This is why He challenges us to worship Him one minute more and give one more thing away in order to be able to move closer to Him.
3. Life becomes a festival rather than a contest because the greatest worship occurs whenever we turn the tables, and our desire is mainly to hear His applause. This is done when we are no longer the audience but instead focus our attention on and perform solely for God.

4. It spills over into our lifestyle and our finances. Why? We begin to appreciate simplicity over the complexity of accumulation. And we must bear it in mind that it is not really ours, so we are not expected to fight over it because it is best given away. Worship is all about seeing the bigger picture of God and the Holy Spirit in truth.
5. We are empowered to see that we are all in our recovery mode because we have become totally "broken down for God."

On the other hand, PRAISE plays a big role in prayer, which is why we must always begin our prayers by praising and thanking God first. The time we devote to asking God for something or presenting our "shopping lists" before Him should be far less than the time we dedicate to praising, thanking and adoring Him. Therefore, what are some of the major effects of praise, if it is that important? They are listed hereunder:

1. It ushers us into God's presence.
2. It opens the gates of Heaven and the doors of blessings.
3. It dissipates worry, dilutes concerns, fear, and sadness and magnifies goodness.
4. It is one of the very bold languages of faith.
5. It capitalizes on who truly matters, God Almighty.
6. It focuses solely on the Lord as the ultimate solution.
7. It brings us so much closer to God.
8. Its absence can stagnate/limit our walk with God and make it impossible to experience Him.
9. It automatically opens one door and closes another. We consequently close the door to the world and press the ignition button to more closeness to the Lord!
10. It is the key to the door of joy, peace, love and faith, which makes it extremely powerful.
11. God inhabits our praises in a tremendous way because He shows Himself in all His glory.

12. The joy and excitement generated during praise are forces to be reckoned with; since, as previously mentioned, it can destroy seen and unseen walls and battles, and it automatically increases anything that seems insufficient!
13. The Holy Spirit instantly begins to strengthen you whenever you begin to praise God from the bottom of your hearts.
14. It is a destroyer of anything negative such as sadness, frustration, fear, and depression, and it makes things new and possible.
15. It magnifies our vision of Jesus by bringing down the enemy and restores our confidence because it is a game-changer.

Before I conclude this chapter, allow me to briefly mention why it is very pertinent to thank God continually. The Bible is filled with numerous references that encourage us to thank God constantly, regardless of our situation. Some of the reasons are:

1. His love endures forever (**Psalm 136:3**)
2. He is always good to us (**Psalm 118:29**)
3. His mercy is everlasting (**Psalm 100:5**)
4. Feeling and expressing appreciation is for our own benefit. Whether we consciously thank Him with faith regarding what we want Him to do or thank Him for His previous goodness to us, we are opening more doors of outpouring blessings and answers to our prayers.
5. It is always in our best interest to realize that everything we have is a gift from Him because, whether by power or might, there is nothing that we can possibly do on our own.
6. Once we omit gratitude and appreciation from our equation with God, we can never arrive at the correct answer!
7. Thankfulness keeps our hearts in good standing with the Giver of all good gifts.

8. Without gratitude, it will look as if we can single-handedly achieve anything on our own and automatically become arrogant in the sight of God.
9. Whenever we begin to thank God for the things that we usually take for granted, our perspective about life changes.
10. By regularly giving thanks to God, we are continually reminded of how much we have and how limited we can be without thanking Him.
11. It makes us happier when we sincerely focus on God's blessings and what He has done for us instead of our wants and expectations.
12. When we are thankful for the things we have and the seemingly difficult and undesirable circumstances, this is when we truly begin to comply with **I Thessalonians 5:18**, which says, *"In everything give thanks"* because this is God's will for us in Christ Jesus.
13. When we deliberately thank Him for everything He allows to come into our lives, we keep bitterness away because it is impossible for thankfulness and bitterness to coexist. We are NOT thanking Him for allowing evil to befall us, but rather we are faithfully thanking Him that He will sustain and see us through (**James 1:12**).
14. We are not thanking Him for the harm He did not cause, but we thank Him when He gives us the strength to endure it (**2 Corinthian 12:9**).
15. We also thank Him for His promise that "All things will work together for good, to those who love God, and are called according to His purpose (**Romans 8:28**).
16. We must always offer and give Him a sacrifice of praises.
17. According to **Philippians 4:6-7**, giving thanks to God keeps our hearts in the right relationship with Him and saves us from a host of harmful emotions and attitudes that will rob us of the peace God wants us to experience continually.

18. **I Chronicles 16:34** says, *"O give thanks unto the Lord, for He is good; for His mercy endureth forever."*
19. Feeling and expressing appreciation is good for us. Like any wise father, God wants us to learn to be thankful for all the gifts He has given to us (**James 1:17**).
20. Gratitude guards against envy because envy makes us want what someone else has. Thus, gratitude enables us to realize that God has given us far more than we deserve.
21. Gratitude defies the wily lies of satan that whispers that God is not good to us.
22. Thankfulness leads to joy! The moment we realize God's abundant goodness and declare it, even during hard and harsh times, we are stepping into the gateway to joy.
23. Thankfulness deepens our faith in God. It helps us to boost our faith when we constantly keep a record of God's past faithfulness. Always remember that on the most challenging days and in the worst circumstances, God's scoresheet of faithfulness is always 100%!
24. Gratitude brings contentment because it makes what we have to look like and become enough. Thus if we are not grateful for what God has given us, getting more would not satisfy us either! Hence, being thankful is the key to contentment.
25. Being thankful brings peace. It is far better to count our blessings and NOT our sheep to get rid of the worry that keeps us awake throughout the night. Gratitude enables us to see that God's hand is all over our circumstances, and whenever we are thankful to Him, He will, in turn, give us supernatural peace.
26. **I Thessalonians 5:16** - *"Rejoice always, pray without ceasing; give thanks in all circumstances for this is the Will of God in Christ Jesus for you."*
27. **Philippians 4:8** - *"Finally, brothers and sisters; whatever is true, what is noble, whatever is right, whatever is pure, whatever is lovely,*

whatever is admirable - if anything is excellent or praiseworthy-think about each thing."

28. **Psalm 106:8-9** - "Let them give thanks to the Lord for His unfailing love and His wonderful deeds for mankind; for He satisfies the thirsty and fills the hungry with good things."

29. **Psalm 100:4** - "Enter his gates with thanksgiving and His courts with praise; give thanks to Him and praise His Name."

30. **Psalm 92:1-3** - "It is good to praise the Lord and make music to your Name, O Most High; proclaiming your love in the morning and your faithfulness at night, to the music of the ten-stringed lyre and the melody of the harp."

31. **Psalm 95:1-3** - "Oh come, let us sing to the Lord; let us make a joyful noise to the rock of our salvation! Let us come into His presence with thanksgiving; let us make a joyful noise to Him with songs of praise! For the Lord is a great God, and a great King above all gods."

32. **Psalm 89:1-2** - "I will sing of the Lord's great love forever, with my mouth I will make your faithfulness known through all generations. I will declare that your love stands firm forever, that you have established your faithfulness in heaven itself."

33. **Psalm 69:30** - "I will praise the Name of God with a song; I will magnify Him with thanksgiving."

34. **Psalm 56:4** - "In God, whose word I praise; in God I trust and am not afraid. What can mere mortals do to me?"

35. **Psalm 28:7** - "The Lord is my strength and my shield; my heart trusts in Him and He helps me. My heart leaps for joy, and with my song I will praise Him."

36. **Hebrews 13:15** - "Through Him then let us continually offer up a sacrifice of praise to God, that is the fruit of lips that acknowledge His Name."

37. **I Chronicles 29:13** - *"And now we thank you, our God and praise your glorious Name."*

38. **I Chronicles 16:23-26** - *"Sing to the Lord all the earth; proclaim His salvation day after day. Declare His glory among the nations, His marvellous deed among all peoples. For great is the Lord and most worthy of praise; He is to be feared above all gods. For all the gods of the Nations are idols, but the Lord made the heavens."*

39. **Psalm 50:14** - *"Offer to God a sacrifice of thanksgiving, and perform your vows to the Most High."*

40. **Jonah 2:9** - *"But I, with shouts of grateful praise, will sacrifice to you. What I have vowed I will make good. I will say, Salvation comes from the Lord."*

41. **Philippians 4:6-7** - *"Do not be anxious for anything, but in every situation by prayer and petition, with thanksgiving, present your requests to God. And the peace of God, which transcends all understanding, will guard your hearts and your minds in Christ Jesus."*

42. **I Timothy 4:4-5** - *"For everything God created is good, and nothing is to be rejected if it is received with thanksgiving, because it is consecrated by the Word of God and prayer."*

43. **2 Corinthians 9:11** - *"You will be enriched in every way so that you can be generous on every occasion, and through us, your generosity will result in thanksgiving to God!"*

44. **I Corinthians 1:4** - *"I always thank God for you because His grace is given to you in Christ Jesus."*

45. **Colossians 4:2** - *"Devote yourselves to prayer, being watchful and thankful."*

46. **Colossians 3:15** - *"Let the peace of Christ rule in your hearts, since as members of one body you were called to peace. And be thankful."*

47. **I Chronicles 16:34-35** - *"Give thanks to the Lord, for He is good; His love endures forever…..and glory in thy praise."*

48. **Ezra 3:11** - "With praise and thanksgiving they sang to the Lord; He is good, His love toward Israel ensues forever. And all the people gave a great shout of praise to the Lord, because the foundation of the house of the Lord was laid."
49. **Psalm 7:17** - "I will give thanks to the Lord because of His righteousness; I will sing the praises of the Name of the Lord Most High."
50. **Psalm 9:1** - "I will give thanks to you Lord, with all my heart; I will tell of all your wonderful deeds."
51. **Psalm 35:18** - "I will give thanks in the great assembly; among the throngs I will praise you."
52. **Psalm 106:1** - "Give thanks to the Lord, for He is good, His love endures forever."
53. **Psalm 107:21-22** - "Let them give thanks to the Lord for His unfailing love and His wonderful deeds for mankind. Let them sacrifice thanks offerings and tell of His works with songs of joy."
54. **Psalm 118:1** - "Give thanks to the Lord, for He is good, for His love endures forever."
55. **Daniel 2:23** - "I thank and praise you, God of my ancestors; you have given me wisdom and power, you have made known to me what we asked of you; you have made known to us the dream of the King."
56. **Hebrews 12:28-29** - "Therefore, since we are receiving a Kingdom that cannot be shaken, let us be thankful and go worship God acceptably with reverence and awe, for our God is a consuming fire."
57. **Psalm 145:18** - "When the peace of Christ rules in our hearts, thankfulness overflows. Even in the darkest of times, we can praise God for His love, His sovereignty, and His promise to be near us when we call."
58. **Psalm 140:13** - "Surely, the righteous shall give thanks unto His name."
59. **Jeremiah 30:19** - "Out of them shall proceed thanksgiving and the voice of them that make merry."
60. **Psalm 68:19** - "Blessed be the Lord, who daily loaded us with benefits."

61. **Psalm 95:2** - *"Come before His presence with thanksgiving."*
62. **I Chronicles 16:8** - *"Give thanks, make known His deeds among the people."*
63. **Luke 6:22-23** - *"When men hate, revile or reproach you, rejoice and praise the Lord."*

Obviously, there are countless biblical references that encourage us always to give thanks and show appreciation to God. I deliberately selected the above for the purpose of brevity. Nevertheless, some common threads that are quite noticeable among all of them are:

1. **Thanksgiving must be expressed irrespective of our situation.**
2. **Gratitude to God is very paramount.**
3. **God's favourable deeds towards us are too numerous to be counted.**
4. **God's kindness towards us is not selective; it has no gender consideration.**
5. **God wants us to thank Him daily and constantly.**

In addition to the various approaches we have discussed so far, we can show gratitude to God in many other ways.

Although it may be difficult for some people, the ultimate way to show gratitude to God is to honour Him with our lives by living according to His will. We can demonstrate this by cultivating a lifestyle of constant prayer, reading His Word (the Bible) and endeavouring to live a life free of sin as much as possible.

Performing acts of service to fellow human beings is another major way of showing appreciation to God. Some people start foundations to assist and help the less privileged in society achieve their purpose in life, especially with their wealth.

Luke 14:11 says, *"For all those who exalt themselves will be humbled, and those who humble themselves will be exalted."* Similarly, Proverbs 22:4 says, *"Humility is the fear of the Lord; its wages are riches and honor and life."* The simple analogy to be drawn from the above references is that once we admit that whatever height or achievement we attain in life was orchestrated by God, we must always humble ourselves before Him.

Talking about showing gratitude to God through service reminds me of I Peter 4:10, which says, *"Each of you should use whatever gifts you have received to serve others; as faithful servants of God's grace in its various forms. If anyone speaks, they should do so as one who speaks the very words of God. If anyone serves, they should do so with the strength God provides, so that in all things God may be praised through Jesus Christ. To Him be all the glory and the power forever and ever, Amen."*

I believe this scripture aptly describes that if we make ourselves vessels for community and social services and offer quality advice to those who require it, with transparent love and companionship, we can show God that we duly appreciate Him.

Therefore, we show gratitude to God by serving Him and His people. The most important thing to remember is to stay consistent for gratitude to become a healthy or regular habit. We must make it a priority to pray for faithfulness daily by asking God to keep us on track and to continuously bring our minds back to the things we are grateful for.

We can give thanks to God for His love even when we cannot readily make reference to specific blessings from Him because I John 4:16 says, *"God is love."* Therefore, no matter what we are passing through, this is something we should try to appreciate sincerely. Even if things are going well for us, we can still pray to God to thank Him for loving us. Immense strength can be generated by giving thanks and praise to God while reminiscing on His good works, and all He has done for us causes our faith to grow more and more each time we give thanks.

For those of you that are opportune to read this book now, God deserves a grateful heart from you because while the young and the old are dying every second throughout the world, you must thank Him for being alive. Thus, we must thank Him daily for good health. If we never made mistakes, we would not learn much. Therefore, it is one of those things we should be thankful for.

God deserves the praises of whoever has the ability to read this book because millions of people worldwide cherish education even at the lowest level but are not opportune to have one. Whether you have a home of your own or are living in a rental, God deserves your gratitude since millions of people don't have anywhere to call home. Many of them are sleeping under the bridge, where rain and sunshine are dealing with them negatively.

Have we ever stopped to think about the fresh air that God gives us freely? Being able to step outside to breathe in fresh air is a good reminder of how many little things we should be thankful for. Having a bed is one of those things that can easily be taken for granted until we do not have one! Also, waking up without immense fear frees us up to really live a good life that deserves gratitude to God.

4

Thanksgiving Days

I was privileged to travel to the United States of America around the time of my birthday in November 1987. A few days after my arrival, we received many guests who visited us to celebrate what they called their "Thanksgiving Day." I can vividly recall that one of the major highlights of the period was the unrestricted consumption of turkey in significant quantities by all and sundry! That was my first time hearing of a country dedicating a special day of the year as "Thanksgiving Day" to really thank and appreciate God for His mercies and benevolence. Upon further inquiry, I was told that it has a historical perspective, and they still observe it till this day as a public holiday. However, I have realized that other countries like Canada, Liberia, Grenada, and the Australian Territory of Norfolk Island also have Thanksgiving Days. Others are China, Germany, Japan and Vietnam.

Although I do not know much about the take-off dates of Thanksgiving Days in other countries, records have it that the American holiday traces its roots all the way back to 1621, when colonists held a harvest feast with local natives.

In 1861, Abraham Lincoln, one of America's former presidents, declared an official Thanksgiving Day in late November. In the 1930's

President, Franklin Roosevelt attempted to move the holiday a few days earlier. But after widespread discontent, he eventually consented to make it an official holiday to be celebrated on the fourth Thursday of November each year.

Over the years, specific traditions and customs associated with the holiday have evolved, from watching afternoon football games to marking the beginning of the holiday shopping season. However, the foundational components of the holiday - celebrating food and the fall harvest and giving thanks with families have remained over time. America seems to be a peculiar country. While citizens of other countries are constantly spewing negative prophecies about their countries, Americans are known for saying "God bless America," although I do not know the origin or what led to this culture.

From the accounts in this chapter, one would note that the above-mentioned countries know the essence of thanksgiving and show gratitude to God. I sincerely opine that this noble idea is one that other countries should fully emulate. I believe that God must have a specific plan in His heart for such countries who have deliberately dedicated a particular day of the year to be thanking Him for one thing or the other. Or what do you think?

Thus, if some Countries could dedicate a special day to thanking God, it behooves us as individuals to sincerely cultivate the conscious habit of regularly thanking man and God for every act of goodness, however great or small. Doing so soothes the nerves of the person being thanked and glorifies God especially.

5

They Also Thanked God

Although we have discussed the three powerful J's (Jesus, Jehoshaphat and Joshua) that applied thanksgiving to bring about very powerful miracles, I wish to briefly make references to some notable Biblical characters who gave thanks to God for what He did.

1. **David:** Whenever most people think of David, they remember him as the youth who killed Goliath, the giant. He was a shepherd boy who became one of the greatest Kings of Israel and is well known for his many Psalms, giving praise and thanksgiving to God. David was a man with a heart after God and of Godly character and integrity. There were times when he failed and sinned, but although he was not perfect, his life was characterized by his love for and his dependence on the Lord. David wrote a multitude of Psalms, many of which contain words of praise and thanksgiving to God and was written in times of distress and trials.

David is an example of someone who continually turned to the Lord in praise and thanksgiving during good times and during trials. This shows that we must also turn to the Lord and trust in Him with thanksgiving and praise whenever we face difficulties.

2. **King Hezekiah:** 2 Chronicles 31:2 tells us, *"And Hezekiah appointed the courses of the priests and the Levites after their courses, every man according to his service; the priests and Levites for burnt offerings and for peace offerings, to minister and to give thanks, and to praise in the gates of the tents of the Lord."*

The nation first began to turn away from God during the reign of King Solomon, the son of King David. However, unlike his predecessors who had forsaken God, Hezekiah, the King of Judah, decided to seek God instead, which resulted in revival and a turning back to the Lord in the nation during his reign. He consecrated the priests and Levites who were not performing their duties and also cleaned and consecrated the Temple. The Passover was celebrated again, which had not been done since the days of Solomon. Idols were torn down, and people began to return to worshiping the true God. Unfortunately, the Nation turned away from following the Lord yet again soon after Hezekiah's death.

3. **Jonah:** In Jonah 2:1, 7-9, the Bible says, *"Then Jonah prayed unto the Lord his God out of the fish's belly. When my soul fainted within me, I remembered the Lord; and my prayer came in unto Thee, unto thine Holy Temple. They that observe lying vanities forsake their own mercy. But I will sacrifice unto thee with the voice of thanksgiving, and I will pray that which I have vowed; Salvation is of the Lord."*

Repulsed by God's call, the Prophet Jonah fled and ended up in the belly of a great fish for his disobedience. Despite being confined in the fish's belly for three days, Jonah did not murmur but instead began to cry out to the Lord. He concluded his prayers by acknowledging that *"Salvation is of the Lord,"* as in Jonah 2:9.

4. **Mariam:** Mariam, the older sister of Moses and Aaron, gave thanks to God while playing her tambourine and dancing with joy with the other women whom God saved from the Egyptians after they crossed the Red Sea (Exodus 15:20-21).

5. **Hannah:** I Samuel 2 details a lengthy prayer of thanks that Hannah recited after God answered her prayers for a son. Once Samuel was weaned, Hannah and her husband, Elkanah, took him to Eli, the priest to be dedicated to the Lord, in accordance with her vow to God.

6. **Elizabeth:** Elizabeth, the mother of John the Baptist, was thankful that God removed her reproach among the people of Israel (Luke 1:24-25). Before becoming pregnant with John, Elizabeth was barren and long beyond child-bearing age.

7. **Mary:** According to Luke 1:46-55, Mary, in a beautiful song of praise known as the Magnificat, gave thanks to the Lord for being chosen to bear the incarnate Son of God.

8. **Paul:** According to Philippians 1:3-11, Apostle Paul gave thanks to God for the believers in Philippi because of their partnership with him in the gospel. And remember that we have discussed several instances in the previous chapters where Paul appreciated God in many magnificent ways during his ministerial assignments.

9. **Daniel:** (Daniel 2:19-23) Since Israel and Judah disobeyed God despite the warnings of the prophets that God sent, God allowed enemy nations to attack them, killing many and carrying away captives. However, during the days of the Babylonian captivity, Daniel followed the Lord despite being a captive and exiled. He attained rank under the reign of King Nebuchadnezzar and favour in the King's sight.

10. **Ezra:** After the destruction of the temple and the Babylonian captivity, some of the Jews returned from Babylon with Ezra. Following the instructions of God, under Ezra's leadership, a new Temple was built. Once the foundation had been laid, a celebration of thanks to the Lord of Israel was made.

Some of the people in Jerusalem who saw Solomon's Temple before its destruction wept when they saw the foundation of the new Temple because it was smaller in size and not as grandiose. But since it was still a special and Holy place for people to worship God, the air was filled with both thanksgiving and weeping on that day.

Hence, according to Ezra 3:10-11, *"And when the builders laid the foundation of the Temple of the Lord, they set the priests in their apparel with trumpets, and the Levites the sons of Asaph with cymbals, to praise the Lord, after the ordinance of King David of Israel. And they sang together by praising and giving thanks unto the Lord; because He is good for His mercy endureth forever towards Israel. And all the people shouted with a great shout when they praised the Lord because the foundation of the house of the Lord was laid."* Some of them lost sight of the joy that the day was supposed to contain. The smaller Temple did not affect who God was. He was and is a good God whose mercies endure forever.

11. **Anna:** In Luke 2:38, *"And she coming in that instant gave thanks likewise unto the Lord, and spoke of Him to all them that looked for redemption in Jerusalem."*

Israel waited for the Messiah for many years. However, it was not until the appointed time that God sent His son, born of a virgin, to be the Savior of the world (Galatians 4:4). Eight days after Jesus' birth, He was dedicated at the Temple, where Anna recognized Him as the

Savior and gave thanks to the Lord. Anna was a Prophetess who stayed in the Temple, serving night and day with fasting and prayers. She had been married for seven years and widowed for the remainder of her eighty-four years. She could have become bitter when her husband died, but instead, she poured herself into the Lord's service (one of the many ways of thanking God, as earlier discussed). Her heart was set on the things of the Lord, and He rewarded her with the sight of the long-awaited Messiah. She did not keep the news to herself but boldly shared it with those who also were waiting for the Redeemer.

12. **King Saul:** According to I Samuel 15:6, King Saul remembered to show appreciation to the foreign tribes for having shown kindness to his forefathers. He instructed the Kenites to quickly leave the vicinity of the Amalekites because he did not want to destroy them also since they had earlier shown kindness to all the Children of Israel when they came up out of Egypt.

13. **Pharoah:** In Genesis 41:39-41, King Pharaoh showed his appreciation to Joseph for having interpreted his dream and for his wise counsel.

14. **Ruth:** In Ruth 3:10, Boaz expressed his appreciation to Ruth for her unselfish devotion when he said, *"Blessed be thou of the Lord, my daughter for thou showed much kindness in the latter end than at the beginning, in as much as thou followed not young men, whether poor or rich."*

15. **King Jeroboam:** In I Kings 13:1-7, the King sincerely appreciated the young prophet who prayed to God that his dried-up hand should be restored.

6

More Thanksgiving References

As I begin to round up this book, I have decided to list some compelling and remarkable Biblical references of thanksgiving for your day-to-day application. I encourage you to continually read them and apply them daily, especially when you remember the contents of Psalm 116:12-14, which says, *"What shall I render unto the Lord for all His benefits towards me? I will take the cup of salvation, and call upon the Name of the Lord. I will pay my vows unto the Lord now, in the presence of all His people."*

I Chronicles 29:10-13 - *"Wherefore David blessed the Lord before all the Congregation, and David said, Blessed be thou, Lord God of Israel our father, forever and ever. Thine, O Lord is the greatness, and the power, and the glory, and the victory and the majesty; for all that is in the heaven and the earth is thine; thine is the Kingdom, O Lord, and thou art exalted as head above all…..Now therefore our God, we thank thee, and praise thy glorious Name."*

Psalm 7:17 - *"I will praise the Lord according to His righteousness, and I will sing praise to the Name of the Lord most high."*

Psalm 26:6-7 - *"I will wash mine hands in innocency, so will I compass thine altar, O Lord. That I may publish with the voice of thanksgiving, and tell of all thy wondrous works."*

Psalm 30:11-12 - *"That hast turned for me my mourning into dancing; thou has put off my sackcloth, and girded me with gladness. To the end that my glory may sing praise to thee, and not be silent. O Lord my God, I will give thanks unto thee forever."*

Psalm 105:1-2 - *"O give thanks unto the Lord; call upon His Name; make known His deeds among the people. Sing unto Him, sing Psalms unto Him; talk ye of all His wondrous works."*

Psalm 136:1-26 (end) - *"O give thanks unto the Lord, for He is good for His mercy endureth forever O give thanks to the Lord of lords for His mercy endureth for ever…..O give thanks unto the Lord God of heaven; for His mercy endureth for ever."*

Psalm 147:1-20 (end) - *"Praise ye the Lord; for it is good to sing praises unto our God, for it is pleasant and praise is comely…..He hath not dealt so with any nation; and as for His judgements, they have not known them; praise ye the Lord."*

Isaiah 12:1-6 (end) - *"And in that day, thou shalt say, O Lord, I will praise thee, though thou was angry with me, thine anger is turned away, and thou comforted me…..cry out and shout; thou inhabitant of Zion; for great is the Holy One of Israel in the midst of thee."*

Amos 4:4-5 - *"Come to Bethel, and transgress; at Gilgal multiply transgression; and bring your sacrifices every morning, and your tithes after three* years. And offer a sacrifice of thanksgiving with leaven, and proclaim and publish the free offerings; for this liketh you, O ye Children of Israel, saith the Lord God."

Jeremiah 30:19 - *"And out of them shall proceed thanksgiving and the voice of them that make merry; and I will multiply them, and they shall not be few; I will also glorify them, and they shall not be few; I will also glorify them, and they shall not be small."*

Jeremiah 33:11 - *" The voice of joy, and the voice of gladness, the voice of the bridegroom, and the voice of the bride, the voice of them that shall say, Praise the Lord of hosts; for the Lord is good, for His mercy endureth forever; and of praise unto the house of the Lord. For I will cause to return the captivity of the land, as at the first, saith the Lord."*

I Corinthians 15:57 - *"But thanks be to God, which giveth us the victory through our Lord Jesus Christ."*

2 Corinthians 2:14 - *"Now thanks be unto God, which always causeth us to triumph in Christ, and maketh manifest the Savior of His Knowledge by us in every place."*

2 Corinthians 4:15 - *"For all things are for your sakes, that the abundant grace might, through the thanksgiving of many, rebound to the glory of God."*

2 Corinthians 9:11 - *"Being enriched in everything to all bountifulness, which causeth through us thanksgiving to God."*

Revelation 11:16-17 - *"And the four and twenty Elders, which sat before God on their seats, fell upon their faces, and worshiped God. Saying, we give* thanks, O Lord God Almighty, which are and wast, and art to come, because thou hast taken to thee thy great power, and has reigned."

Ruth 2:12 - "The Lord recompense thy work, and a full reward be given thee of the Lord God of Israel, under whose wings thou are come to trust."

Nehemiah 12:46 - "And both the singers and the porters kept the ward of their God, and the ward of the purification, according to the Commandment of David, and of Solomon, his son."

Ephesians 1:6 - "To the praise of the glory of His grace, wherein He hath made us accepted in the beloved."

Ephesians 5:19-20 - "Speaking to yourselves in Psalms and hymns and spiritual songs, singing and making melody in your heart to the Lord. Giving thanks always for all things unto God and the Father in the Name of our Lord Jesus Christ."

Psalm 106:1 - "Praise ye the Lord, O give thanks unto the Lord; for He is good, for His mercy endureth forever."

Job 1:21 - "And said, Naked came I out of my mother's womb, and naked shall I return thither: the Lord gave and the Lord hath taken away; blessed be the Name of the Lord."

Psalm 16:6-7 - "The lines are fallen unto me in pleasant places; yea, I have a goodly heritage. I will bless the Lord, who hath given me counsel; my reins also instruct me in the night seasons."

Psalm 34:1-22 (end) - "I will bless the Lord at all times; His praise shall continually be in my mouth. My soul shall make her boast in the Lord; the *humble shall hear thereof and be glad…..The Lord redeemeth the soul of His servants; and none of them that trust in Him shall be desolate."*

Please, permit me to say that the last Golden Verse above (Psalm 34) is one of my personal favourite Psalms. I greatly recommend that you acquaint yourself with the entire chapter, especially if you have never come across it before because it will be one that you will come to love.

7

The Dangers of Ingratitude

Months before I began to write this book along with three others simultaneously, the outlines had already been boldly written and laid out. At that time, I never thought that I would delve into "ingratitude or ungratefulness" separately and treat it as a chapter. Sincerely speaking, this golden idea dropped into my heart while writing down item 23 of the previous chapter in the manuscript! And who am I to ignore God's instruction when He said, *"Your chapter remains one; tell your readers about ungratefulness because many of them don't know that I hate it."*

The Bible says much about gratitude as well as the lack thereof. God knows exactly how we are made and has designed us to thrive when we are humble, thankful, appreciative, and of good morals. Therefore, when we are arrogant, immoral and ungrateful, we cannot have warm fellowship with Him, nor can we experience what it truly means to be created in the image of God according to Genesis 1:27, James 4:6 and I Peter 5:5.

Thus, God included repeated commands in His Word about being thankful and reminding us that a grateful heart is always a happy heart (I Thessalonians 5:18, Colossians 3:15 and Psalm 105:1).

Ingratitude is a sin with very severe repercussions. Romans 1:18-32 gives a detailed description of the downfall of a person or a society that fails to appreciate God and states that every kind of rebellion is unthankfulness. Verse 21 shows us that God takes both gratefulness and ungratefulness seriously, *"Although they knew God, they neither glorified Him as God, nor gave thanks to Him."*

As long as a person or a culture remains thankful to God, they retain sensitivity to His presence. Hence, thankfulness toward God requires a belief in God at the very least. At the same time, ingratitude fails to fulfill our responsibility to acknowledge Him (Proverbs 3:5-6 & Psalm 100:4). When we refuse to be thankful or fail to express gratitude, we grow hard-hearted and become proud. We then take all that God has given to us for granted and become our own gods.

As discussed in the previous chapters, Jesus' healing of the ten lepers gives us a powerful example of how highly God values thankfulness (Luke 12:12-19). Jesus healed all of them, but only one returned to thank Him (Verse 15). The Bible specifically tells us that the thankful leper was not even a Jew but a Samaritan, which demonstrated that Jews were not only the people who could reach the heart of God.

The Lord takes note of those who thank Him, irrespective of socio-political standing or level of spirituality. So, for Him to have said in Verse 17, *"Were not all ten cleansed? Where are the other nine?"* concretely showed His disappointment towards the ingratitude of the remaining nine. And as mentioned in Chapter 1 of this book, this was why I used the illustration of these lepers as one of the overarching principles and templates for writing this book!

2 Timothy 3:2 describes what people would be like in the last days, and one evident characteristic is ingratitude. When pride and self-rule become fashionable, the human heart has no one to thank, not even God! We become convinced of our own supremacy and consider all we have as a just reward for our personal efforts. It would therefore be wise to heed Paul's rhetorical questions, *"What do you have that you did not receive? And if you did indeed receive it, why do you boast as though you did not?"* (I Corinthians 4:7)

Ingratitude toward God is not so much a cause of evil but the result of it. Once we have hardened our hearts to the point that we no longer see God as the source of our gifts, nothing is off-limits, and we become a law unto ourselves. And God knows that the end result of arrogance is a reproachable mind (Romans 1:24). Thus, whenever we remind ourselves that all we are and all we have is a gift from God (James 1:17), we are guarding ourselves against pride and idolatry.

Let me quickly share with you some solid Biblical references about ingratitude:

1. **2 Timothy 3:2** - *"For people will be lovers of self, lovers of money, proud, arrogant, abusive, disobedient to their parents, ungrateful and unholy."*
2. **Proverbs 17:13** - *"If anyone returns evil for good, evil will not depart from his house."*
3. **Genesis 40:23** - *"Yet the chief cupbearer did not remember Joseph, but forgot him."*
4. **Hebrews 12:28** - *"Therefore let us be grateful for receiving a Kingdom that cannot be shaken, and thus let us offer to God, acceptable worship, with reverence and awe."*

5. **Romans 1:21** - *"For although they knew God, they did not honour Him as God, nor give thanks to Him, but they became futile in their thinking, and their foolish hearts were darkened."*
6. **Colossians 3:17** - *"And whatever you do, in word or deed, do everything in the Name of the Lord Jesus, giving thanks to God the Father through Him."*
7. **Psalm 38:20** - *"Those who render me evil for good accuse me because I follow after good."*
8. **Psalm 7:4-5** - *"If I have repaid my friend with evil or plundered my enemy without cause, let the enemy pursue my soul and overtake it; and let him ramble my life to the ground and lay my glory in the dust, Selah."*
9. **2 Chronicles 24:22** - *"Thus, Joash the king did not remember the kindness that Jehoiada, Zechariah's father, had shown him, but killed his son. And when he was dying, he said, "May the Lord see and avenge."*
10. **I Samuel 25:21** - *"Now David had said, "Surely in vain have I guarded all that this fellow has in the wilderness, so that nothing was missed of all that belonged to him, and he has returned me evil for good."*
11. **Psalm 35:12-13** - *"They repay me evil for good; my soul is bereft. But when they were sick, I wore sackcloth; I afflicted myself with fasting; I prayed with bowed head on my chest."*
12. **Psalm 109:4** - *"In return for my love they accuse me, but I give myself to prayer."*
13. **2 Corinthians 12:15** - *"I will most gladly spend and be spent for your souls. If I love you more, am I to be loved less?"*
14. **Jeremiah 18:20-21** - *"Should good be repaid with evil? Yet they have dug a pit for my life. Remember how I stood before you to speak good for them, to turn away your wrath from them. Therefore, deliver up their children to famine; give them over to the power of the sword; let*

their wives become childless and widowed. May their men meet death by pestilence, their youths be struck by the sword in battle."

15. **Ecclesiastes 9:15** - "But there was found in it a poor, wise man, and he by his wisdom delivered the City. Yet no one remembers that poor man."

16. **Psalm 38:1** - "My friends and companions stand aloof from my plague, and my nearest kin stand far off."

17. **Job 19:14-16** - "My relatives have failed me; my close friends have forgotten me. The guests in my house and my maidservants count me as a stranger; I have become a foreigner in their eyes. I call to my servant, but he gives me no answer; I must plead with him with my mouth for mercy."

18. **I Samuel 24:17** - "He said to David, "You are more righteous than I, for you have repaid me good, whereas I have repaid you evil."

19. **Genesis 31:6-7** - "You know that I have served your father with all my strength, yet your father has cheated me and changed my wages ten times. But God did not permit him to harm me."

20. **Malachi 1:6** - "A son honors his father, and a servant his master. If then I am a father, where is my honor? And if I am a master, where is my fear? Says the Lord of Hosts to you, O priests who despise my name. But you say "How have we despised your Name?"

21. **Psalm 50:23** - "The one who offers thanksgiving as his sacrifice glorifies me; to one who orders his ways rightly I will show the salvation of God."

22. **Judges 8:35** - "And they did not show steadfast love to the family of Jerubbaal (that is Gideon) in return for all the good that he had done to Israel."

23. **Ephesians 2:8-9** - "For by Grace, you have been saved through faith. And this is not your own doing; it is the gift of God and not as a result of your works, so that no one may boast."

24. **Deuteronomy 33:18** - *"You were unmindful of the Rock that bore you, and you forgot the God who gave you birth?"*
25. **Numbers 16:3** - *"They assembled themselves together against Moses and Aaron and said to them, "You have gone too far! For all in the congregation are holy, every one of them, and the Lord is among them. Why then do you exalt yourselves above the assembly of the Lord?"*
26. **Exodus 16:3** - *"And the people of Israel said to them, "Would that we had died by the hand of the Lord in the land of Egypt, when we sat by the meat pots and ate bread to the full, for you have brought us out into this wilderness to kill this whole assembly with hunger."*

Therefore, based on everything we discussed in this chapter, it is clear that God detests ungratefulness and strongly admonishes us to be grateful at all times, to both Him and man, as contained in Psalm 107:8, *"O that men would praise the Lord for His goodness, and for His wonderful works to the Children of Men."*

8

Don't Murmur, God Hates it

After discussing gratefulness elaborately and briefly touching on ingratitude, I felt the urge to conclude this book with a brief discussion about murmuring. A deep insight would show that all 3 of them are connected and interrelated in a big way. In an ideal situation and form, murmuring was supposed to be dealt with in a separate book entirely. Still, I decided to include it here because of its compatibility with thankfulness and ingratitude.

For any discerning believer, whenever the word "murmuring" is mentioned, the event of the Israelites in the wilderness (Numbers 14:1-3) would easily come to mind. It says, *"so all the Congregation lifted up their voices and cried, and the people wept that night! And all the children of Israel complained against Moses and Aaron, and the whole congregation said to them " If only we had died in the land of Egypt! Or if only we had died in the wilderness! Why has the Lord brought us to this land to fall by the sword, that our wives and children should become victims? Would it not be better for us to return to Egypt?"*

The Israelites murmured against their gracious and loving God in the above text, which seriously displeased Him.

To murmur means to grumble or whine. Although complaining in and of itself is not inherently wrong, especially when deemed necessary to bring lasting progress to a situation, it should still not warrant murmuring since this is viewed as a sin by God. Sadly, many Christians fall into the category of murmurers and complainers. Many people are found grumbling, murmuring, and/or complaining at home, on the job, within the neighbourhood and even in the church. Why? They fail to see anything good concerning their lives, business, career, health, and future. For most, everything seems bleak, miserable and full of discomfort: and they find it very difficult to understand why they should be grateful and thankful to God concerning anything about their lives.

The Jews murmured against Jesus Christ because He said He was the Bread of Life (John 6:41). Instead of finding out what He meant by that statement in order to understand Him, they murmured. The Scribes and the Pharisees murmured against the disciples of Jesus Christ because they ate and drank with publicans and sinners, but they were really aiming at the Lord (Luke 5:29-32)! They weren't concerned that the publicans and the sinners equally needed Jesus Christ because they were too focused on their personal agenda. The Bible says in Philippians 2:14-15 that we should *"Do all things without complaining or disputing, that you may become blameless and harmless children of God without fault in the midst of a crooked and perverse generation among whom you shine as lights in the world."* Therefore, we should be as hospitable as possible to one another without grumbling (I Peter 4:9) because it causes one to perish. And herein lies the corollary. Whoever fails to remain thankful to God could ultimately perish.

Selfishness is another major of murmuring according to Philippians 2:4 and Romans 15:2. Selfish people usually want to have their own way with everything and seriously detest it if they do not get it and consequently begin to murmur. They are never content with whatever they have. In fact, they don't even believe that they have anything, talkless of appreciating it.

In Numbers 14:27, the Bible says, *"How long shall I bear with this evil congregation, which murmur against me? I have heard the murmuring of the Children of Israel, which they murmur against me."* God outrightly calls the sinful spirit of murmuring, grumbling and complaining against Him as outright REBELLION. He accused them of testing and despising Him ten times, and on each occasion, they refused to repent. In Deuteronomy 1:27, the Bible says, "And ye murmured in your tents, and said, *"Because the Lord hated us, he hath brought us forth out of the land of Egypt, to deliver us into the hands of the Amorites, to destroy us."* The same action of the Israelites is described in Psalm 106:24-26 thus, *"Yea, they despised the pleasant land, they believed not His word! But murmured in their tents, and hearkened not unto the voice of the Lord. Therefore He lifted up His hand against them, to overthrow them in the wilderness."*

Complaints come from the fleshy nature of our hearts and rob us of God's blessings and visible grace. Complaining could arise from various sources, some of which include:

1. **Comparison and self-pity** (Numbers 11:1-3)
2. **Hate**
3. **Ingratitude**
4. **Deficiency of the Holy Spirit**
5. **Greed**

Therefore, a complainer is anyone who is always discontented with his lot in life, and it is certainly not a fruit of the Spirit (Galatians

5:22-23). It is quite detrimental to the peace, joy and patience that usually comes from the spirit and is very destructive and debilitating personally, making our witness to the world more difficult.

Adam was the first complainer who, after he and Eve disobeyed, complained to God, "*The woman you put here with me gave me some fruits from the tree, and I ate it*" (Genesis 3:12). His son, Cain, also complained. However, undoubtedly within himself (Genesis 4:6). Moses too complained to God when he met Him in the burning bush (Exodus 3:4). Moses again repeatedly complained about deliverance from the Israelites, grumbling and Idolatry (Exodus 17:4 & 32:31-32). At the same time, David the Psalmist also offered up to the Lord (Psalms 2:1, 12:1-2, & 22:1).

If we grumble and complain, it shows how worldly we still are (James 4:1-3). A complaining spirit leads to fighting and quarrelling because complaints come from unfulfilled desires, which could lead to envy and strife, as shown in Genesis 37:3, concerning the story of Joseph and his brothers.

Thus, it is quite evident from all of the preceding that whoever is deficient in appreciating God and what He has done for them will ultimately fail to show gratitude to Him. Anybody that fails to realize that many people are constantly striving to be like him or catch up with him can never be grateful to God and will continue to grumble or murmur against God, and He hates it because He will always view it as a sin.

At this juncture, let me share some references from the Bible that clearly show us that grumbling and murmuring are both sinful to God, and hated by Him, viz:

1. **I Corinthians 10:10-11** - *"Nor grumble as some did and were destroyed by the Destroyer. Now these things happened to them as an*

example but they were written down for our instruction, on whom the end of the ages has come."

2. **I Peter 4:9** - *"Show hospitality to one another without grumbling."*
3. **Colossians 3:8** - *"But now you must put them all away: anger, wrath, malice, slander and obscene talk from your mouth."*
4. **Deuteronomy 32:5** - *"They have dealt corruptly with Him; they are no longer His children because they are blemished; they are a crooked and twisted generation."*
5. **Ephesians 4:29** - *"Let no corrupting talk come out of your mouths, but only such as is good for building up, as fits the occasion that it may give grace to those who hear."*
6. **Exodus 15:24** - *"And the people grumbled against Moses, saying what shall we drink?"*
7. **Exodus 16:7** - *"And in the morning you shall see the glory of the Lord, because He has heard your grumbling against the Lord. For what are we that you stumble against us?"*
8. **Genesis 3:12** - *"The man said, "The woman whom you gave to be with me, she gave me the fruit of the tree, and I ate it."*
9. **James 5:9** - *"Do not grumble against one another, brothers, so that you may not be judged; behold, the judge is standing at the door."*
10. **Job 1:22** - *"In all this, Job did not sin or charge God with wrong."*
11. **Job 2:10** - *"But he said to her, "You speak as one of the foolish women would speak. Shall we receive good from God, and shall we not receive evil?" In all this, Job did not sin with his lips."*
12. **John 6:41** - *"So the Jews grumble about Him because He said 'I am the bread that came down from heaven."*
13. **John 6:61** - *"But Jesus, knowing in Himself that His disciples were grumbling about this, said to them, "Do you take offense at this?"*

14. **Luke 5:30** - "And the Pharisees and their Scribes grumbled at His Disciples, saying, *"Why do you eat and drink with tax collectors and sinners?"*
15. **Numbers 14:27** - *"How long shall this wicked congregation grumble against me? I have heard the grumblings of the people of Israel, which they grumble against me."*
16. **Proverbs 13:10** - *"By insolence comes nothing but strife, but with those who take advice is wisdom."*
17. **Romans 1:21** - *"For although they knew God, they did not honor Him as God, or give thanks to Him, but they became futile in their thinking, and their foolish hearts were darkened."*
18. **Romans 12:2** - *"Do not be conformed to this world, but be transformed by the renewal of your. Mind, that by testing you, may discern what is the will of God, what is good and acceptable and perfect."*
19. **Proverbs 19:3** - *"When a man's folly brings his way to ruin, his heart rages against the Lord."*

From all that we discussed in Chapter 1 of this book, you would agree with me that it is essential to sincerely cultivate the constant habit of showing appreciation for any act of kindness that one receives. Gratitude must be shown to both God and man, as doing so could open more channels of favour or as assistance in future from any quarrels.

Acts of ungratefulness or ingratitude should be avoided at all costs because the Bible completely condemns them.

On the other hand, murmuring or grumbling is seen by God as a sin because it shows that whoever does that does not appreciate God at all. All should cultivate PAT (Praise, Appreciation & Thanksgiving).

A Sinner's Prayer

Dear Heavenly Father,

I come to You in the Name of Jesus Christ.

You said in Your Word, "Whosoever shall call upon the name of the Lord shall be saved" (Romans 10:13). I am calling on Your Name, so I know You have saved me now.

You also said that "if you confess with your mouth the Lord Jesus and believe in your heart that God has raised Him from the dead, you will be saved. For with the heart one believes unto righteousness, and with the mouth, confession is made unto salvation" (Romans 10:9-10). I believe in my heart Jesus Christ is the Son of God. I believe that He was raised from the dead for my justification, and I confess Him now as my Lord and Savior.

Thank you, Lord, because now, I am saved!

Thank You, Lord, because I know you have heard my prayer. Thank You, Lord, because I am now born again.

Signed _____

Date _____

About the Author

Apostle Dr. Victor Adekunle Adewusi was a passionate Spiritual Leader and Father of many children and grandchildren.

He was also the Author of five books *"The Secrets of Happy Parenting," "Control Your Anger," "Praise, Appreciation & Thanksgiving (PAT)," "Mine Shall Be Done,"* and *"Fear Not, Cheer Up, Do Not Despair."*

Until his passing, he was the General Overseer of The Eternal Sacred Order of The Cherubim and Seraphim Church, Oke Ibukun Branco; The Governor of the Yabatech Class of 1986 governing council; a Member of The Chartered Institute of Management; A Fellow of The Chartered Institute of Taxation of Nigeria and A Fellow of The Institute of Chartered Accountants of Nigeria (ICAN).

Apostle Dr. Victor Adekunle, who was a philanthropist, has drawn on his personal breakthrough life experiences to help people overcome challenges and attain greater achievements in their life.

www.ingramcontent.com/pod-product-compliance
Lightning Source LLC
Chambersburg PA
CBHW070342010526
44107CB00004B/591